Bayou Born

Exploring Creole Identity

by
Jwanna Savoie-Powell

Table of Contents

Introduction:
A Glimpse into Creole Life

To immerse oneself in Creole life is to dive deep into a rich tapestry of cultural intricacies and historical depth that has, for centuries, thrived in the heart of Louisiana. The term 'Creole' itself is both vibrant and ambiguous; it defies static definition, for its identity is rooted in a past that is as complex as it is fascinating. The Creole culture of Louisiana is a syncretism of the French, African, Spanish, and Native American influences, masterfully weaving together a society that retains its unique flair and robust spirit against the backdrop of the American narrative.

The essence of Creole life—its customs, traditions, and ethos—has evolved over time, carrying legacies that span the period of European colonization through the epochs of slavery and emancipation to the ever-shifting present. The Creoles of Louisiana offer more than a mere study of historical consequence; they are a people whose daily practices, language, and artistry reflect a particular worldview, born not simply of geographical location but of the confluence of human struggles, triumphs, and resilient adaptation.

This introduction serves as a siren's call to the curious and the scholarly alike, beckoning you to discover the soulful essence of Creole culture. Be prepared for a journey that will not only inform, but captivate, as you traverse through narratives of music, gastronomy, spirituality, and language that are not merely aspects of culture but the lifeblood of Creole identity.

The origins of Creole culture herald back to an era when Louisiana was a melting pot of European colonial ambitions and the forced migration of Africans. Echoes of this past resonate in the modern Creole society, which still embraces its historical origins while perpetually redefining itself within a modern framework.

As we step momentarily into the world of language, it is imperative to understand that Creole dialects extend beyond the realm of communication—they are a force that shapes community identity, that carries memories from one generation to the next through every inflection, phrase, and lilting rhythm. When we later explore Creole French, it won't solely be from a linguistic perspective, but rather as a component of the Creole essence itself.

Culinary traditions in Creole life serve not only to nourish but to tell the stories of those who have stirred the pots before, blending indigenous ingredients with imported tastes to create dishes that are both historical documents and living phenomena. However, we will delve deeper into signature dishes and gastronomic roots in dedicated subsequent sections of this book.

The cadence of life here is often set to the beats of Zydeco and Cajun music, merging the energy of African rhythms with the soul of French ballads and the spirit of the bayous. Creole music, steeped in the history of diverse peoples, acts as both a timeline and a contemporary festival of everyday life. Dance too, as we shall learn, is more than movement; it is a physical manifestation of a deep-seated cultural heritage.

Our travels through Creole life cannot be complete without touching upon the rich vein of folklore and spirituality that runs beneath the observable surface. Enigmatic tales emerge from the bayou, while spiritual practices manifest in syncretized forms, blending the transcendental with the ancestral. These rich narratives and beliefs are the stewards of values, the gatekeepers of the Creole ethos.

The impressions left by Creole culture on art and literature form the collective memory of a people both celebrated and misrepresented, a duality that has yielded a complex portrayal in the wider sphere of American culture. The creativity inherent in Creole society is as palpable today as it was in the whispered stories of yesteryear, finding expressions in manifold forms that continue to haunt and inspire.

As we endeavor to sketch a portrait of Creole life, we recognize that this endeavor is akin to capturing a river's current—fluid, ever-changing, and filled with the reflections of those who gaze upon it. It is a life that eludes simplicity, for its beauty lies within its undulating nuances and the depth of its historical currents.

Though this section does not venture into exhaustive detail about the chronicle of Louisiana's Creole population or the specifics of their evolutions, it is crucial to underscore that the many facets we will examine are interwoven strands of a single narrative. Each piece is essential to the whole, contributing to an understanding that is vibrant in its complexity and rich in its storytelling.

The overarching goal of this book is to present a dignified and intimate glimpse into the lives of the Creole people, honoring both their shared heritage and individual experiences. We aspire to elevate understanding and appreciation, to set the stage for the celebration and preservation of a culture that forms an invaluable piece of both Louisiana's and America's patchwork identity.

Now, as we turn the pages of this journey through Creole life, let it be with open minds and a readiness to encounter a world where tradition meets vitality, where memory intertwines with the pulse of the present, and where every corner turned reveals another layer of the rich Creole experience. Welcome to a world that is at once historical and contemporary, both familiar and intriguingly other.

This book is your atlas through this vibrant cultural landscape, guiding you not by the strict lines of the historian's map, but rather through the colorful pathways that are trodden daily by those who call

Creole culture their home. May this introduction lead you with anticipation into the deeper explorations of subsequent chapters, where the Creole life is painted in broader strokes, on a canvas that is both vivid and exquisite to behold.

Chapter 1:
Origins and Evolution

Having delved into the vibrant tableau of Creole life, it's crucial to trace the roots of this unique cultural mosaic. The origins of Louisiana's Creole population emanate from a rich tapestry of ethnicities and nationalities, a convergence of French, Spanish, African, and Native American influences, each contributing to the fabric of what would become a distinct cultural identity. The evolution of this population didn't follow a linear trajectory; rather, it twisted and turned through history's manifold vicissitudes. From the early settlements in the 18th century to the shifting social strata brought on by wars, trade, and legal transformations, Louisiana's Creole population has constantly adapted, preserving some traditions while embracing new influences. Such historical dynamics have not only shaped the demographic landscape but also sowed the seeds of a cultural metamorphosis that has continued to characterize Louisiana's social and cultural milieu.

The Early History of Louisiana's Creole Population

The mosaic of cultures that is Louisiana today can't be appreciated without delving into the complex origins of its Creole population. The term 'Creole' is derived from the Portuguese word 'crioulo', which originally referred to people of European descent born in the colonies. Over time, in the context of Louisiana, Creole came to encompass a broader, more nuanced spectrum of identities, encompassing persons of mixed European, African, and Indigenous American heritage.

The genesis of Louisiana's Creole population can be traced back to the early 18th century. The French were the initial colonial powers to lay claim to the region, with the establishment of the French Louisiana territory. To expeditalize the development of this nascent colony, the French brought in settlers from their own country, as well as from other regions such as Canada, known at the time as Acadia. These settlers would become the ancestors of the Louisiana Creoles.

Alongside European settlers, the early Creole identity was forged in the fires of the transatlantic slave trade. Africans, primarily from West and Central Africa, were forcibly brought to Louisiana to labor on sugar and indigo plantations. These Africans did not merely contribute their labor; they brought with them rich traditions, languages, and religious beliefs which deeply infused the evolving Creole culture.

Frequently overlooked but equally integral to the Creole tapestry were the Indigenous American tribes, such as the Choctaw, Houma, and Chitimacha. Through intermarriage and cultural exchange, their influence melded with European and African traditions to create a distinct Creole syncretism reflected in language, food, and a shared cultural ethos.

Amid this confluence of cultures, colonial Louisiana became a space of both oppressive hierarchy and exceptional fluidity. While the French imposed strict codes to maintain societal order, a degree of social mobility was available to the Creole population, particularly for those of mixed race, who often found themselves in intermediate social positions. The 'Code Noir', although primarily oppressive, inadvertently allowed for a unique legacy of mixed-race Creoles who later played a pivotal role in the cultural development of the region.

The latter part of the 18th century brought significant change when Louisiana transitioned from French to Spanish control. The

Spanish colonial regime introduced its own complexities to the already intricate Creole identity. With the arrival of Spaniards and Canary Islanders, or 'Isleos', further layers were added to the Creole cultural quilt, with lasting impacts particularly visible in architecture and gastronomy.

During the late 1700s and early 1800s, the Creole population also swelled due to the influx of refugees from the Haitian Revolution. White and free people of color, along with enslaved Africans, fled the turmoil in Saint-Domingue, bringing with them elements of French Caribbean culture which quickly assimilated into Louisiana's Creole milieu.

As the United States acquired Louisiana through the Louisiana Purchase in 1803, the Creole population faced yet another cultural shift. The introduction of Anglo-American laws, language, and customs further reshaped Creole society. Despite the imposition of the English language and other American norms, the Creole population held fast to their Francophone traditions and cultural practices, reinforcing their distinct identity within the broader tapestry of American society.

Throughout the 19th century, the concept of Creole identity continued to evolve as New Orleans emerged as a cultural and commercial hub. The city became the heartbeat of Creole life, where free people of color often enjoyed a level of affluence and education not seen elsewhere in the antebellum South. The term Creole began to signify not just one's ethnic background but also an attitude, a cultural stance linked with urban life, sophistication, and self-assurance.

The Civil War and the end of slavery brought significant transformations to Louisiana's Creole population. In the postbellum period, the Jim Crow laws and the American binary racial system challenged the fluidity of Creole identity. As Creoles were increasingly categorized as black under segregationist laws, many aspects of Creole culture became part of the broader African American experience.

The early 20th century saw a renaissance in Creole self-awareness as there was a resurgence of interest in preserving French language and Creole customs. This period witnessed a flourish of literary and artistic works that celebrated and reflected upon Creole heritage—an effort to conserve a unique world-view amid the pressures of Americanization and modernization.

As we pore over the annals of Louisiana's history, we see that the early Creole population formed the bedrock for a dynamic and distinctive culture. Their narratives are not mere footnotes but integral chapters in the story of a state that stands as a testament to cultural resilience and hybridity. The rich tapestry woven by the Creoles in these formative years established the core of what is now recognized as Louisiana's vibrant Creole tradition—a tradition that endures and morphs even in contemporary times.

Thus, the early history of Louisiana's Creole population is a testament to the strength and creativity born of diverse influences blending under sometimes harmonious, often contentious circumstances. The survival and evolution of Creole culture defy easy categorization or summary. It is a history that encompasses great complexity and beauty, as well as pain and resilience. From its earliest days, Louisiana's Creole population charted a path of cultural synthesis that continues to echo through the streets of New Orleans and the bayous of the countryside, a melody of heritage played out through centuries.

The legacy of the early Creole population cannot be overstated; this rich cultural heritage continues to shape the identity of Louisiana to this day. As we transition to exploring the evolution of Louisiana's Creole population, it becomes clear that the foundations laid by this diverse collective of individuals provided the framework for the continuous growth and adaptation of Creole culture. Understanding their early history is crucial to appreciating the depth and breadth of the Creole identity that remains an indelible part of Louisiana's soul.

The Evolution of Louisiana's Creole Population The narrative of Louisiana's Creole community is enveloped in layers of migration, cultural amalgamation, and socioeconomic changes. From its genesis under French and Spanish colonial rule, the term 'Creole' has undergone significant transformations, each marked by historical milestones that have shaped the state's demographics to this present day. The complexity of this evolution is integral to understanding the tapestry of identities within Louisiana.

In the early stages of Louisiana's colonization, 'Creole' referred principally to Europeans born in the New World, distinct from those born in their home countries. However, as African slaves were brought to work on the burgeoning sugarcane and rice plantations, their descendants, born in Louisiana, also came to be known as Creoles. Thus, the term initially indicative of geography began to acquire ethnic and cultural connotations.

The Creole population diversified further with each new arrival on Louisiana's shores. Africans from various regions, with disparate cultures and languages, mingled with the Indigenous peoples of the area, French settlers, and later, Spaniards who took control of the territory following the secret Treaty of Fontainebleau in 1762. This amalgamation gave birth to a unique Creole culture characterized by its blend of customs, beliefs, and practices.

By the late 1700s and into the 1800s, the Haitian Revolution had a substantial impact on Louisiana's Creole population. The upheaval propelled a significant migration of white planters, free people of color, and enslaved Africans from Saint-Domingue to Louisiana. These immigrants, known as the Saint-Domingue refugees, further enriched Creole society with their influences, strengthening the French-Creole traditions in the process.

As America expanded its territories, Louisiana's 1803 acquisition through the Louisiana Purchase introduced Anglo-American legal and cultural norms. This exposure precipitated another shift in the meaning of 'Creole,' which began to distinguish the older populations of French and Spanish descent from the newer Anglo arrivals. Here, the term Creole began to encapsulate resistance, a holding onto the old European way of life in the face of the encroaching American culture.

The antebellum period saw a sharpening of racial divides within the Creole population. While the term had long included both white and black Creoles, social stratification intensified with the implementation of more stringent racial laws. The caste system of the time recognized free people of color, many of whom were Creoles and enjoyed some rights and privileges, which were nevertheless incomparable to their white counterparts.

The abolition of slavery and the end of the Civil War brought drastic changes to the social fabric of Louisiana. Freed African Americans, including those with Creole heritage, faced a new reality of redefining their place in society. During Reconstruction, the lines between different Creole identities blurred as the fight for civil rights and equality took precedence.

Entering the 20th century, Creoles confronted the Jim Crow laws that enforced racial segregation and further complicated Creole self-identity. The Plessy v. Ferguson decision of 1896, initiated by a Louisiana Creole of color, Homer Plessy, became a landmark case in the struggle against these segregationist policies. Amidst this oppression, Creoles of color forged community resilience, focusing on education, entrepreneurship, and the reinforcement of cultural pride.

The Great Depression and the two World Wars brought economic turmoil and social upheaval, which led to significant internal migrations. Many Louisiana Creoles, especially those in rural areas, moved to urban centers like New Orleans for better opportunities. This urban migration created new interactions and exchanges between rural Creole customs and urban traditions.

As the civil rights movement gained momentum during the mid-20th century, many Creoles of color found themselves aligning with broader African American struggles, yet their unique cultural heritage was often at risk of being overshadowed by the larger narrative of racial equality. Despite this, there persisted a strong undercurrent of Creole cultural maintenance and revival efforts.

In recent decades, the Creole identity in Louisiana has witnessed a resurgence of interest and pride. The late 20th and early 21st centuries have seen increased efforts to celebrate Creole heritage, from festivals and historical symposia to academic studies and culinary tourism. Today's Creoles often embrace a multicultural, multiracial identity that honors their diverse heritage and reflects the dynamic history of Louisiana.

Presently, the term Creole continues to evolve, mirroring the global trends of cultural hybridity and interaction. In an age of awareness about the importance of preserving cultural identity, Louisiana's Creole population remains steadfast in its commitment to celebrating their unique history and traditions even as they adapt to contemporary societal changes.

Given the nuanced history of Louisiana's Creoles, their trajectory is a testament to the enduring spirit of a people forged through centuries of convergence and adaptation. Their story is one of survival, resilience, and an unyielding dedication to the preservation of a heritage that transcends simple racial or ethnic categorization.

The Creole experience in Louisiana serves as a profound illustration of how cultures can intertwine, forging a transcendent identity that carries the wisdom of the past into the innovations of the future. As we delve deeper into the chapters ahead, the language, cuisine, music, spirituality, and artistic contributions of the Creoles will further illuminate how profoundly this unique population has shaped, and continues to shape, the cultural landscape of Louisiana.

Chapter 2:
Language of the Bayou

The cadence of Louisiana's Creole population is as much a tapestry of sound as it is a marker of identity. In the heart of the bayous, language isn't just a method of communication; it's the lifeblood of community, a cherished heirloom passed down through generations, and a testament to resilience. Key to understanding this culture is immersing oneself in Louisiana Creole French—a linguistic blend of French, African, Spanish, and Native American influences that embodies the region's diverse history. As we drift through the whispers of the willows and the chatter of marketplaces, the unique lingo reveals itself: an intricate dialect that carries with it the joys, sorrows, and enduring spirit of the Creole people. It's not just words that define the language of the Bayou, but the stories they tell, the bonds they forge, and the traditions they uphold. Here, every greeting, jest, and piece of wisdom shared over a simmering pot of gumbo is enameled with the patina of ages—an enthralling lexicon shared by those who can't help but translate their vibrant culture into the richly textured stanzas of everyday conversation.

Understanding Louisiana Creole French is not merely an exercise in linguistic prowess but a gateway into the heart of Louisiana's Creole culture. This unique dialect is a testament to the region's rich history, a melting pot of French, African, Spanish, and Native American influences. Efforts to describe Creole French requires one to tread a path that meanders through the bayous and time, revealing a language that has evolved significantly from its European roots.

First and foremost, Louisiana Creole French, or simply Creole, differs from the more widely known Cajun French, although they share a geographical home and external perceptions often conflate the two. Creole emerged among the descendants of African slaves and free people of color, forged from the intermingling of European settlers, primarily the French, with enslaved Africans and indigenous tribes. This contact language incorporated words, syntax, and sounds from each group's native tongues, creating a linguistic mosaic that perfectly illustrates the diverse human tapestry of early Louisiana.

In the past, Creole was spoken throughout Louisiana, serving as the lingua franca in a multilingual society. However, its prominence has faded in the face of English dominance, leading to its classification as an endangered language. Preservationists today fight to ensure its survival through educational programs, literature, and media.

The language itself, with its variable grammar structures, can be puzzling to French speakers unfamiliar with its idiosyncrasies. Pronunciation in Creole French can be quite different; for example, the nasal sounds prevalent in standard French are softened, and the rhythm of speech is more akin to African and Caribbean cadences.

An aspect of Creole that illustrates the blend of cultures is its vocabulary, which borrows liberally from African languages, primarily from the regions from which the enslaved people came. These African words are so thoroughly incorporated that many speakers may not be aware of their origins. Words for common objects, foods, and everyday activities often reflect this unique linguistic blend.

The verb forms in Creole French are simplified compared to standard French. For instance, verb conjugation is minimal, and the use of auxiliary verbs is much less common. This simplicity in structure is a trait shared by many creole languages and is often what gives them a distinct flair and charm among linguists and language enthusiasts.

Community events and familial gatherings often showcase the vitality of Creole French. Being primarily oral in nature, the language has a strong tradition of storytelling, which serves as both entertainment and a method of passing down history and customs across generations. These stories are rich tapestries woven with moral lessons, humor, and cultural references unique to the Creole experience.

Importantly, Louisiana Creole French is not static; it continues to evolve even as it holds onto the past. While the number of fluent speakers may be declining, there is a resurgence of interest among younger generations who view the language as a critical piece of their heritage.

Despite its evolution and the influence of English, Creole French remains an integral part of the local identity in Louisiana. The language is a badge of pride for those who speak it and a beacon for those curious about this distinct culture.

The comparison between Creole French and standard French is not merely linguistic but cultural. Creole is informal, intimate, and filled with expressions that reflect the laid-back attitude toward life that is characteristic of Louisiana. These colloquialisms paint pictures of Creole life that are not easily translated into any language, including standard French.

Efforts to document and study Louisiana Creole French have been undertaken by scholars and activists alike. Their work includes compiling dictionaries, recording oral histories, and even developing online resources for language learning. These endeavors are not just academic; they are acts of cultural preservation.

Audibly, Creole French is rapidly recognized by its unique accent, marked by a certain musicality. It is a dialect that breathes life into thre

French language and adds a distinctly American flavor, resisting the homogenization that often comes with globalization.

Understanding Louisiana Creole French thus transcends grammar and phonetics—it is an appreciation for the complexity and resilience of a people and their language against the backdrop of a storied history. It is an ode to the persistence of culture through the modality of speech.

To fully appreciate this language is to embrace the broader context of the Creole experience in Louisiana. It's not just a means of communication but also an art form that has endured despite challenges to its existence. Creole French acts as a living museum, preserving the past and yet still evolving, revealing its layers to those who wish to explore the depths of Louisiana's cultural heritage.

It is within this dialect that one can find the heartbeats of those who came before, the songs of the bayou, and the whispers of the Louisiana wind. Learning about, and striving to understand, Creole French offers more than a linguistic endeavor; it is a journey through time, an act of preservation, and a deep dive into the soul of the Creole community. In the intricate dance of words and expressions lies the truth of the Creole spirit, resilient and unyielding.

The Role of Language in Creole Identity Language, as the philosopher Ludwig Wittgenstein once intimated, is the limit of one's world. For the Creoles of Louisiana, language is not only a communicative tool but a cornerstone of cultural identity. In a region where history swirls through the streets like the Mississippi River, the Creole language is a tapestry of social, political, and racial intricacies— an audible legacy of the era when Europe danced with Africa upon the soil of the New World.

In Louisiana, the term "Creole" can encompass varied ethnicities and backgrounds, but historically, it refers to the descendants of French and Spanish settlers, African slaves, and Native Americans. This melding of cultures has birthed a unique linguistic phenomenon:

Louisiana Creole French. A creole language, rich with its mix of vocabulary and grammatical structures, is often the linguistic embodiment of a people who are themselves defined by the convergence of disparate heritages.

It's crucial to parse that Creole, as a linguistic term, does not merely mean 'a mix.' In the world of linguistics, a "creole" language emerges when a pidgin, developed among speakers of different languages for basic communication, becomes the first language of a community and develops a more complex system that allows for full expressive capacity. Louisiana Creole French is precisely this—a language born out of necessity that has matured into a medium of cultural cohesion.

The language is as flavorful as the region's cuisine, rich with tones and phrases that can't be found elsewhere. Within its linguistic codes are encoded the memories of the past—of times both turbulent and tranquil. When a Creole speaks, the history of Louisiana speaks with them, in an accent colored by the French but inflected by Africa and the Caribbean.

Historically, social and legal structures aimed at segregating and demoralizing enslaved people stripped away many aspects of African heritage, including language. Yet, the will to retain identity was stronger. Creole, fertile in its ability to absorb and retain, kept alive the essence of the languages and customs that might otherwise have been lost to time and oppression. In Creole speech, the heartbeats of various African languages still resonate beneath the French-derived syntax.

However, the significance of the language goes beyond historical remnants. In contemporary Louisiana, speaking Creole can be a political act—a deliberate statement of identity and heritage. Amid the forces of globalization and the homogenizing influence of the English language, to choose Creole is often to choose resistance against cultural erosion.

The influence of language on identity is further felt in community cohesion. In many Creole communities, language acts as a gatekeeper, defining who belongs and who stands outside. A shared language forges a bond among speakers, creating a sense of "us" that is powerful and deep-rooted. For Louisiana Creoles, French is a line connecting the present with the annals of ancestry, and speaking it is akin to evoking the spirits of forebears.

Fluency in the Creole language serves not only as a form of historical and cultural connection but also as an instrument of education. Within families, it's a vehicle for passing down traditions, stories, and values. The language embraces within it myriad lessons of resilience, of adaptation, and of the strength found in diversity. Each phrase and proverb is a lesson from the past, imparting wisdom and reflecting community values.

This binding identity through language is even manifest in the arts. Much like the Creole language, which is an amalgam of different linguistic traditions, Creole music and literature are syntheses of various artistic traditions. Understanding the Creole language offers a richer appreciation for these genres, each word resonating with layers of meaning and history not readily apparent to the non-speaker.

Language revitalization efforts also underscore the role of language in maintaining Creole identity. As Louisiana Creole French has been endangered by the dominance of English, these initiatives endeavor to reclaim not just words but identity. Language classes, cultural programs, and local movements are increasingly becoming arenas for re-establishing the prominence of this cultural treasure.

Also in education, where English predominates, speaking Creole within the home grounds children in their heritage. It's a living link to an identity that transcends the four walls of a classroom. For Creole children, language is a way to understand where they come from and to shape where they decide to go. It's not just a form of communication but a compass for cultural navigation.

Within the broader scope of American society, where the concept of "melting pot" culture often assumes assimilation, the ability to maintain a distinct language signifies more than just linguistic preference—it represents a form of cultural resilience and a resolve to preserve a unique identity.

The Creole language plays a pivotal role in the realm of social interactions and relationships within the culture itself. Intimate expressions, humor, and everyday colloquialisms in Creole foster a sense of intimacy and cultural specificity that bond individuals within the community. Language offers a shared space where the nuances of Creole life are felt and intimately understood.

Despite the encroaching forces of linguistic homogenization, the Creole language remains a defiant standard-bearer of a rich heritage. Through festivals, gatherings, and daily speech, the language thrives as a marker of Creole identity, encapsulating a rich, nuanced history that refuses to be forgotten. Speaking Creole is not just a nostalgic nod to the past; it is a vibrant testament to a living, evolving culture.

Thus, the interweaving of language and identity among Louisiana's Creoles is an emphatic affirmation of who they are and whence they came. In a changing world, where languages and traditions face extinction, Louisiana Creole remains a rebellious whisper of the past, drastically shaping the fabric of the present and audaciously assuring its resonance into the future. That is the enduring power and role of language in Creole identity—an unyielding echo of self amidst the symphony of human diversity.

Chapter 3:
Culinary Traditions

The tapestry of Creole culture is richly woven with tantalizing flavors and time-honored recipes that tell the story of a diverse people and their relationship with the land. The culinary practices within Louisiana's Creole communities are the fruition of a unique confluence of French, African, Spanish, and Native American influences; they encapsulate a history that's as complex as the flavors on the plate. The Creole kitchen itself is a canvas for a resourceful cooking style that emphasizes local ingredients like crawfish, okra, and sassafras—building blocks of a cuisine that's inherently tied to the region's bountiful ecosystem. Each dish, from the hearty gumbo to the indulgent beignets, carries with it generations of tradition and serves as a testament to the resilience and creativity of the Creole people. With each simmering pot, there's an unspoken narrative, weaving the past with the present and filling the air with the aromatic promise of shared heritage and continuity.

The Flavors of Creole Cuisine As the narrative moves from an exploration of identity and language, the journey delves into the fascinating realm of Creole cuisine. It is here we encounter a culinary tradition steeped in history, marked by a confluence of cultures that is as complex as the Creole population itself. The essence of Creole cooking lies not just in its techniques or ingredients, but also in its capacity to tell the story of the people and the place from which it originates.

Creole cuisine is a sophisticated blend, reflecting the diverse heritage of the Louisiana Creole population. It's a testament to the mix of French, Spanish, African, Native American, and Caribbean influences that have come together to create a unique and rich gastronomic tapestry. The Creole kitchen is one that honors the past while continuously evolving, charging each dish with a deep sense of place and tradition.

The fundamental flavors of Creole cuisine are often referred to as the "holy trinity," where onion, celery, and bell pepper form the foundational base for many dishes. This aromatic trio, akin to the French mirepoix, sets the stage for a symphony of flavors, with garlic, thyme, bay leaves, and parsley contributing to the complex undertones. Creole dishes frequently showcase such depth, resulting from slow cooking and careful layering of spices.

Talking about spices, it's hard to discuss Creole cuisine without acknowledging the pivotal role of file; powder and spices like cayenne, which are indispensable parts of the Creole pantry. File, made from dried and ground sassafras leaves, is commonly used to thicken and flavor stews and gumbos. The heat from cayenne and other peppers isn't just about spice; it's about adding vibrancy and excitement to the palate.

A distinction often arises between Creole and Cajun cuisines, although outsiders frequently conflate the two. Creole cooking, characteristically found in New Orleans, typically features more tomatoes and often employs butter and cream, echoing European influences. It is seen as somewhat more urbane and refined compared to its rustic Cajun cousin, which finds its roots in the rural parts of Louisiana.

Rice also plays a starring role in Creole dishes, serving as more than just an accompaniment. It absorbs the rich array of flavors in dishes like jambalaya, a one-pot meal with Spanish and French roots, and etouffee, a thick and hearty stew that is simmered slowly to perfection.

Seafood is a vital component of this cuisine, given Louisiana's abundance of fresh shrimp, crab, oysters, and fish from its Gulf waters. Classic Creole seafood preparations often feature a roux-based sauce, thickened with flour and fat, indigenous to French culinary traditions. A great example is the well-known shrimp creole, where the seafood is simmered gently in a piquant tomato sauce replete with the holy trinity and a generous helping of spices.

The influence of African culinary traditions can't be overlooked, with okra featuring prominently in Creole cooking. This vegetable, brought by African slaves, is central to gumbo—a dish that is perhaps the epitome of Creole culinary syncretism. Okra not only adds flavor but also acts as a thickening agent, testifying to the innovative use of local ingredients.

When it comes to desserts, Creole cuisine is just as rich and varied. French-inspired desserts like beignets, a type of square-shaped doughnut covered with powdered sugar, are iconic. Equally significant are desserts like bread pudding, sweet potato pie, and pralines—each with a history that mirrors the fusion of cultures within Creole society.

If one were to sum up the spirit of Creole cuisine, it would be its hospitality and emphasis on communal dining. Meals are often lavish affairs meant to be shared, whether it's a large pot of gumbo or a platter of red beans and rice—a reflection of the Creole emphasis on family and communal ties.

Moreover, the seasonings used reflect the cuisine's adaptability and ingenuity, with local ingredients such as pecans, mirlitons (chayote squash), and Andouille sausage frequently showcased. Take, for example, the Creole mustard—a condiment that's sharp with an almost horseradish-like heat, which perfectly complements the robust flavors of the cuisine.

Cocktails also find their place in the Creole culinary experience, with creations like the Sazerac and the Hurricane becoming synonymous with New Orleans' vibrant food scene. The mingling of spirits with local flavors speaks to a culture that celebrates life with joie de vivre and adds an extra dimension to the Creole table.

In essence, the flavors of Creole cuisine are a dialogue between the old world and the new, between local produce and global influence. This is a cuisine that does not just rely on the quality of its ingredients or the precision of its techniques, but rather, on the connections it embodies—ties that bind people, places, and histories together in each savory bite.

As the epicurean exploration progresses, it is vital to understand that Creole cuisine is not just about the food itself, but also the interplay of cultural dynamics that give rise to such a distinctive and beloved culinary genre. Each dish tells a story, each flavor carries a legacy—making the act of dining a nourishing experience, both for the body and the spirit.

While this section has introduced the palate to the broad strokes of Creole flavors, the succeeding subsection will delve further into actual dishes that define Creole cuisine. From the iconic gumbo to the lesser-known yet equally delectable maque choux, the culinary narrative of Creole culture continues, dish by dish, recipe by recipe.

Signature Dishes and Their Historical Roots The odyssey into Creole culture would remain incomplete without a thoughtful immersion into its cuisine – a delectable tapestry of flavors that narrates the history of a people through each sumptuous bite. Louisiana's culinary traditions are a robust celebration of its diverse origins; a fusion of French, Spanish, African, and Native American influences that have mingled over centuries to form the bedrock of Creole cooking.

The hallmark of Creole cooking is the reverence for fresh, local ingredients coupled with intricate techniques passed down through generations. Rumored to be the first North American region to have learned advanced culinary arts from the French, this epicurean heritage boasts of dishes that are as storied as they are flavorsome.

Jambalaya stands as a robust pillar of the Creole culinary landscape. Its origin can be traced to both French and Spanish ancestors of the region, mirroring the paella of Spain and the jambalaia of the French Provincial regions. The dish is a hearty concoction that ingeniously mixes rice with a variety of proteins, from the sea's bounty of shrimp and crawfish to the earthy offerings of andouille sausage and chicken, all simmered with the holy trinity of Creole cooking: bell peppers, onions, and celery.

Gumbo, with its roux-darkened depths, is another emblematic Creole creation, born out of a confluence of culinary practices. With West African slaves contributing okra as a thickening agent, to the Choctaw's file; powder, and the French's technique of roux preparation, gumbo epitomizes the melting pot symbolism that is at the heart of Creole culture. Each variant, from seafood to chicken and sausage, tells the tale of resourcefulness and adaptability of Creole cooks.

Red beans and rice also hold a special place within the Creole culinary repertoire. Traditionally served on Mondays using the Sunday ham bone for flavor, this humble dish flaunts the Creole ability to turn simple ingredients into comfort food. Its roots can be found in the West African custom of cooking beans and rice seasoned with leftover meats, showcasing how Creole cuisine turned a day of laundry into a delicious, slow-cooked tradition.

If ever there was a contest for a dish that could represent the luxury of Creole cuisine, Oysters Rockefeller would be a gilt-edged contender. Its birthplace, the famous Antoine's Restaurant in New Orleans, speaks volumes about the innovation within the Creole kitchen. Invented in the early 1900s and named after one of the wealthiest Americans at the time for its richness, this dish elegantly combines fresh oysters with a sauce of pureed greens and breadcrumbs, broiled to perfection.

Beignets, the quintessential New Orleans treat, are the Creole answer to the fritter, albeit with a French touch. These light, square pastries, laden with powdered sugar, can be traced back to French colonists who brought with them the choux pastry technique. Today, these pillows of sweetness have become synonymous with the French Quarter and the relaxed pace of Creole indulgence.

The Crawfish étouffée is yet another culinary masterpiece that captures the essence of Creole innovation. This stew, centered around the tender tails of crawfish, is thickened to a luxurious velvet texture. It's a rich blend of Native American spice and French cooking philosophy, simmered patiently, and usually served over rice, most traditionally during the crawfish season that spans from late winter to early summer.

Shrimp Creole highlights the Creole kitchen's love affair with seafood, drawing upon both Caribbean and African influences. The dish features plump Gulf shrimp simmered in a tomato-based sauce with the holy trinity, garlic, and spices. Its simplicity defies the depth of its flavor, emblematic of the Creole capacity to elevate local produce to culinary prominence.

Bananas Foster, a more recent addition to the Creole palate, came to life in the post-war glamour of the 1950s. Created at Brennan's Restaurant in New Orleans, it was a way to utilize the surplus of bananas being funneled into the port. Sautéed in butter, brown sugar, cinnamon, and rum, and served flambé, the essence of this dish characterizes the jubilant spirit of Creole dining and its enduring appeal for theatrical presentation.

The humble but crowd-pleasing Po' boy sandwich is deeply ingrained in the blue-collar history of New Orleans. Conceived during a streetcar strike in 1929, this generous sandwich was originally filled with fried potatoes and roast beef gravy and offered for free to the "poor boys" on the picket line. Over time, the Po' boy has evolved, often featuring fried seafood, and remains a beloved symbol of the Creole spirit of community and solidarity.

Muffuletta, with its layers of capicola, mortadella, salami, mozzarella, provolone, and the crucial olive salad, is another testament to the multicultural melting pot of Creole cuisine. Italian immigrants in the French Quarter devised this meaty, savory sandwich, which has become an integral part of the local food scene, representing the assimilative nature of Creole cultural and culinary identity.

Creole cream cheese, a byproduct of the dairy industry that French settlers brought over, is a testament to the affinity for dairy craftsmanship within the Creole tradition. This luscious cheese, traditionally served with fruit or sugar, became a farmhouse staple and is now experiencing a revival as a heritage food, symbolizing Creole cuisine's richness and diverse influences.

Last, but by no means least, the iconic King Cake, associated with Mardi Gras festivities, encapsulates the spirit of Creole celebrations. With its roots in European carnival traditions, the King Cake was embraced by the Creole community, who transformed it with local touches like cinnamon-laced brioche, cream cheese fillings, and festive purple, green, and gold sugar, each color holding its own significance. This cake is not just a dessert—it's a vibrant participant in Creole revelry, complete with a hidden figurine that marks the finder as royalty for a day or obligates them to continue the party by hosting the next King Cake event.

Each of these dishes has a narrative deeply embedded in the local soil, the gulf waters, and the historical tapestry of Louisiana. Whenever Creoles gather for a meal, they partake not only of the food laid out before them but also of the rich legacy of their ancestors. Thus, Creole cuisine serves as a medium, a historical record, and a profound communal experience, grounding each participant in the story of their shared past, even as they add to its continuing history.

As one traverses through the flavor-scapes of these signature dishes, it becomes evident that the heart of Creole cuisine lies in its connection to the past. Each spice blend, each cooking method, and each community gathering is a testament to the dynamic, ever-evolving Creole identity. These dishes are not just meals; they are heritage and history on a plate, whispering tales of times bygone and continuously shaping the vibrant living culture of the Louisianan Creole people.

Chapter 4:
Creole Music and Dance

After a savory venture through the culinary heartland of Creole tradition, Chapter 4 dives into the vibrant realms of music and dance, quintessential expressions of Creole joie de vivre. Infused with the pulsating rhythms of Zydeco and the melodic contours of Cajun tunes, Creole music serves as both a historical chronicle and a living, breathing embodiment of a culture in constant conversation with its roots and the wider world. Dance floors across Louisiana become hallowed ground where intricate footwork and communal celebration transcend the mere act of dance, reinforcing social bonds and continuing an ancestral legacy. As these art forms echo across generations, they carry the stories, struggles, and jubilations of a people whose artistic contributions have left an indelible mark on the cultural landscape not only of Louisiana but of the entire United States. This chapter casts a spotlight on how these practices have shaped Creole identity and how, through each note played and step taken, the spirit of an entire community comes alive, ensuring the beat goes on in the heart of Creole country.

The Rhythms of Zydeco and Cajun Music Despite their common roots, Zydeco and Cajun music evolve distinctly as they serve as the vibrant backdrop to Creole culture in Louisiana. Zydeco, derived from the French phrase 'Les haricots,' which means 'the beans,' reflects the music's humble beginnings among sharecroppers and the rural working class. The very essence of Zydeco pulses with the hardships and celebrations of life, blending sounds that are both soulful and life-affirming.

Zydeco music is an eclectic fusion of French Creole tunes, blues, and rhythm and blues, featuring the distinctive sound of the accordion paired with the washboard, or frottoir. To understand this rhythm is to appreciate its driving beat, which compels the body to move with an almost involuntary response. It is the quintessential sound of Creole parties and family gatherings, where dancing and music intertwine for hours on end.

Cajun music, while sharing some instrumental similarity with Zydeco, such as the presence of the accordion, has its own unique sound. It is often characterized by the melancholic fiddle and the presence of French lyrics sung in the hauntingly raw style that echoes the experiences of the Acadian people – their sorrows, their joys, and their resilient spirit. The rhythm is steady but can also quicken to a lively tempo, encouraging a spirited two-step dance.

The historical roots of these musical styles merge with the narrative of Creoles in Louisiana, encapsulating their heritage. Zydeco particularly resonates with the African-American segment of the Creole population, while Cajun music is closely related to the white Cajuns of French Canadian descent. Yet, both styles have acted as cultural bridges, leading to shared experiences among diverse communities throughout the region.

The instruments that are pivotal in these genres hold significant cultural implications. The accordion in Zydeco, for instance, is not just a musical apparatus; it is a symbol of the Creole's adaptation and improvisation. Originally brought by European immigrants, the accordion was embraced and integrated into the Creoles' musical repertoire, representing the amalgamation of different cultures.

The frottoir, or rub-board, fashioned from washboards and played with spoons or thimbles, adds further texture to the sound of Zydeco. It exemplifies the ingenuity of turning everyday objects into instruments, carving out an unmistakable rhythm that is both a historical remnant and a musical innovation.

In Cajun music, the fiddle is often a focal point, its plaintive tones pulling at listeners' heartstrings. It's an instrument of storytelling, capable of conveying the emotional depth of Creole life through its melodies. Meanwhile, the presence of the accordion in Cajun music, though similar to Zydeco, has a distinct style of play, with Celtic and Old World influences perceptible in its sound.

Both Zydeco and Cajun music frequently incorporate call-and-response patterns, a testament to their African and Native American influences. This interactive aspect of the music forges a bond between performer and listener, dissolving barriers and knitting the community more tightly together during performances.

Lyrically, songs in both genres often address themes common to Creole life: love, loss, history, and the sociopolitical issues of the day. In Zydeco, the lyrics might be sung in English, sprinkled with Creole French phrases, speaking to experiences of migration, struggle, and celebration. Cajun songs, traditionally performed in French, serve as the archive of the Cajun experience, preserving history and heritage through oral storytelling.

Zydeco, in particular, has seen a surge in popularity beyond the boundaries of Louisiana, finding its way into urban clubs and international festivals. It's a style that continually evolves, infusing elements of modern genres like hip-hop and soul, which keeps it fresh and relevant. Cajun music also has experienced a renaissance, and bands and music festivals have done much to bring this compelling sound to a global audience.

The rhythmical structure of both Zydeco and Cajun music is crucial to the accompanying dance forms. The quick-paced two-step or the more leisurely waltz that accompanies Cajun tunes provide not just an avenue for enjoyment but also a means of cultural preservation and transmission. Similarly, Zydeco dance, characterized by its fluidity and syncopation, is not just a form of entertainment but a vessel of history and identity.

The essence of these music genres lies not only in the notes and the words but also in their capacity to unify. Zydeco festivals and Cajun fais do-do (dance parties) are more than mere social gatherings. They are communal events where young and old, novice and experienced, come together in celebration of Creole culture, manifesting a spirit of inclusiveness and shared joy.

In light of their importance, Zydeco and Cajun music have been recognized by institutions such as the Grammy Awards, which added categories for both genres. This represents an acknowledgment of their influence and contributions to the musical tapestry not only of Louisiana but of the world.

The audial tapestry woven by the rhythms of Zydeco and Cajun music is as intricate and colorful as the Creole culture itself. Each accordion squeeze, frottoir scrape, and fiddle draw becomes a thread in the broader context of communal identity, history, and the unyielding spirit of the Louisiana Creoles.

The lively beats of these music genres invite one to step into a world where past and present coalesce, where every chord and chorus tells a story. They don't just represent a genre; they are the heartbeat of a rich cultural legacy, continuing to shape the Creole narrative through vibrant rhythms and resonant themes.

Dance as a Cultural Expression in Creole Life Pivotal to the understanding of any culture is the recognition of its dance, a vibrant tableau which enacts the stories, emotions, and communal bonds that text alone cannot convey. In the animated world of Louisiana's Creoles, dance serves as a spirited chronicle, unfolding the nuances of identity, resilience, and joy that have sustained this unique community through the centuries. Culled from a rich tapestry of African, French, Spanish, and Native American influences, the Creole dance tradition is at once a historical record and a living, pulsating gesture of life.

When the Creole population emerged from the eclectic mix of races and backgrounds, so too did an expressive culture that reveled in music and dance. Dance formed a core element of Creole celebrations, whether during grand balls in the oak-canopied estates of the French Quarter or amidst the more rustic gatherings on the back porches of bayou cottages. These social events were held as testament to Creole endurance and communal coherence, with dance steps passed down through generations like treasured heirlooms.

One cannot delve into this subject without acknowledging the famed Louisiana ballrooms of the 18th and 19th centuries. Here, the minuet and the quadrille were not just dances but social institutions, prescribing the etiquette and the societal structures that dictated Creole social life. It was within these hallowed halls that young Creoles learned to navigate their society with grace and agility, negotiating complex patterns that mimicked the intricacies of Creole societal relations.

Dancing in Creole culture often unfolded in tandem with music, be it the rousing melodies of a fiddle or the pounding syncopation of a Cajun accordion. Zydeco, emblematic of the Creole musical tradition, provides the perfect backdrop for exploration of Creole dance expression. The "rub-board" or frottoir, washboard vest played alongside the accordion, gifts a rasping, percussive heartbeat to the dance, prompting bodies to move with a certain frisson unique to Zydeco gatherings.

Across the stretch of festive occasions, the Creole waltz would often take center stage. Unlike the European variant, which emphasizes poise and reserve, the Creole waltz is infused with an earthier, more impassioned tempo. Close embrace and eye contact bridge the distance between the dancers, their steps resonating with the intimacy and the spirited independence that underpins Creole life.

The two-step, another dance form within the Creole repertoire, demands mention. Though simple in structure, this traditional dance demands a deep connection to the rhythm and an understanding of one's partner, weaving a dialogue between two persons that transcends mere physical movement. In Creole society, the two-step served as a social barometer, a means for individuals to engage publicly with tradition and community.

The 'juré' dance, possessed of a more informal, spontaneous character, reveals another facet of Creole dance expression. Rooted in African tradition, 'juré' is often performed to call-and-response singing, with no musical instruments to guide the movements. Here, dance serves as the primary communicative mode, narrating tales of toil, love, and the ever-present Creole wit.

Within this realm of culture, dance workshops and community events sustain the legacy of Creole dance. These gatherings are as much about learning and perfecting steps as they are about instilling a sense of identity and continuity in successive generations. Instructors—often carriers of their craft through direct lineage—teach not just the motions but the history and significance behind them, ensuring the dance remains both an artistry and a historiography.

Creole dance does not exist in a vacuum. It is invariably tied to the Mardi Gras festivities, a time when the Creole community, alongside other residents of Louisiana, parades and dances with unbridled exuberance. Masked balls and street dances become a melting pot of Creole expression, overlaying traditional steps with contemporary flair—thus rearticulating historical dance forms into present-day jubilation.

At weddings, christenings, and even funerals, dance remains a linchpin of ceremonial observances. It's a communal embrace, a collective nod to the life event being honored. Funerary processions, somber in their essence, often culminate in vibrant dance-offs, the 'Second Line' processions where sorrow is danced away in an affirmation of life's continuum and the undying spirit of the Creole ethos.

Creole dance has also found its place within the educational sphere where it acts as a tool for cultural transmission. School programs and local community initiatives include Creole dance as part of their curriculum, not only to keep tradition alive but also to imbue young Creoles with a palpable connection to their heritage. These endeavours stress the relevance of dance in understanding one's roots and fostering pride in a shared cultural narrative.

As the sun sets on the bayou and the fiddles tune up for an evening's revelry, dance floors fill with the graceful and lively steps of Creoles young and old. It's here, in the very swish of skirts and the tapping of feet upon weathered wood, that one grasps the enduring essence of Creole life. Beyond the mere rhythm and steps, dance articulates the visceral joy of a people whose culture is a vivid dance of endurance against the odds of history.

Moreover, the impact of Creole dance has rippled outwards, transcending regional boundaries to influence broader American dance customs. The infectious rhythms, the communal excitement, and the storytelling inherent in the dance have captivated audiences and dancers far beyond Louisiana, contributing a distinctive vibrancy to the national dance tapestry.

As Creole culture continues to evolve, so too does its dance, breathing in contemporary influences while exhaling its storied past. Dancers may fuse hip-hop with two-step or jazz with Zydeco, experimenting with form while maintaining the soulful connection with Creole rhythms. Such innovations ensure that Creole dance remains a living language, one that speaks of a people's past and their unwavering presence in the annals of American cultural expression.

The story of Creole dance is not static; it's a tale in constant motion, swayed by the winds of change yet anchored deeply in the fertile Louisiana soil. In this dance of history and modernity, of roots and revolution, Creole life pirouettes resiliently, telling its story footstep by footstep, spin by spin, to anyone willing to join the floor and partake in its enduring legacy.

Chapter 5:
Creole Folklore and Spirituality

Moving beyond the pulsating rhythms explored in the previous chapter, Chapter 5 delves into the mystical realms that have deeply influenced Creole culture. Creole folklore and spirituality emanate from a rich tapestry of African, Native American, and European traditions, melding to form a unique cultural phenomenon. This chapter will unveil the captivating folktales that have been whispered through the marshes and moonlit fields of Louisiana for generations, narratives filled with creatures of legend, cautionary tales, and ancestral wisdom. Furthermore, it will explore the profound spiritual dimension of Creole life, where the practice of Voodoo, with its African origins, coexists and intertwines with Catholicism, a vestige of European colonization. The resultant syncretism is a vivid tableau of rituals, beliefs, and practices that are central to Creole identity and that continue to shape the community's shared experience and perception of the world around them.

Tales from the Bayou: Folklore and Myth

The murky waters of Louisiana's bayous are as rich in folklore as they are in biodiversity. Louisiana's Creole culture, a vibrant tapestry woven from French, African, Spanish, and Native American threads, is particularly steeped in tales that span the spectral to the celebratory. To traverse this ethereal landscape is to walk amidst legends, some whispered on the winds since time immemorial, others as recent as the memory of an elder in the village square.

Perhaps the most iconic of these bayou legends is that of the Rougarou, a beast as integral to Louisiana folklore as the werewolf is to the mythologies of Europe. Variously described as a cursed individual or a shape-shifting creature, the Rougarou is feared for its penchant for roaming the swamps at night, preying on the wayward and disobedient. In whispers, parents recount the legend to their children, fostering both a respect for the natural domain and a warning against the ills of transgression.

Another captivating figure is the Feufollet, or "Will-o'-the-Wisp," a mysterious light that flickers over the marshes and lures the unsuspecting deeper into the realm of the unknown. Tales spun around the Feufollet are often allegorical, a physical manifestation of the siren songs that call one away from the path of righteousness into realms of lost souls and mischief.

Equally enthralling are the stories of Loup-garou, a variant of the Rougarou, with its origins possibly predating the arrival of Europeans, a dire wolf of indigenous myth that has since melded with French werewolf lore. These tales, emblematic of the complexities of Creole identity, are simultaneously unique to the bayou and universal in their ancient archetypes of transformation and wildness.

More benign, but no less fascinating, are the legends of the Cauchemar, a night-spirit or hag that sits upon the chests of sleeping victims, suffocating them into the terror of sleep paralysis. Whispered accounts of endurance and warding off the Cauchemar are as much a commentary on the power of faith as they are on the darker shades of the human experience.

Then there are the tales of lovers reunited and torn asunder. One such romance is the heartbreaking story of the Ghostly Lovers of Bayou Sale, where the spirit of a young woman eternally searches the fog-laden swamps for her lost beau, both having met tragic demises on the eve of their elopement. It's a story that has serenaded many souls to lament over love as eternal and unyielding as the bayou itself.

Folklore is not merely about the mysterious creatures and the haunting spirits, but also about the veneration of natural phenomena. The Bonfires of the Levees—a blending of French Christmas traditions with African and Haitian practices—herald the Christmas Eve in many Creole communities. While rooted in Christian lore, the practice is also a way to honor ancestors and light the way for Papa Noël (Father Christmas).

Amidst these traditional myths and legends, more contemporary tales have taken root in the consciousness of Creole culture. Historical figures, such as the pirate Jean Lafitte, have transcended their mortal lives to become enshrined in the annals of bayou folklore. Lafitte, the swashbuckler and smuggler, is oft depicted in stories as a Robin Hood of the swamps—his hidden treasure still the subject of many a whispered conversation in the taverns of old Louisiana towns.

These stories and more form the backbone of bayou culture, an intricate blend of the natural and the supernatural, the historical and the proverbial. They echo the syncopated rhythm of the bayou itself— a world in which life and death, joy and sorrow, and the earthly and ethereal waltz in an endless embrace.

Understanding the pull of these tales is to grasp the Creole way of co-existing with the land and water that nourish and threaten life in equal measure. To the uninitiated, they may seem like mere superstitions, but in the heart of Louisiana, they are the narrative threads that bind the communities to their past and to one another. These stories, passed down across generations, reflect the deep respect for nature, the interdependence of life, and the ever-present ghosts of history that walk among the living.

The oral tradition of storytelling imbues continuity into the oft-fluid identity of the Creole people. In the recounting of each myth, a re-affirmation of shared values and ancestry is steadfastly replicated.

These tales contribute to communal cohesion, preserving a unique way of life that has survived through colonialism, slavery, and the inexorable march of time.

It is in the embrace of these stories that the Creole culture stands resilient against the homogenizing forces of the contemporary world. A culture once suppressed, now increasingly celebrated, finds its heart in the stories of the bayou—a testament to the endurance and adaptability of its people. As Creole culture continues to evolve, it does so with the knowledge that folklore and myth are not relics of the past, but living entities that continue to shape the collective consciousness.

The legends explored in this section are an invitation to peer beyond the veil of the physical world and into the rich psychic fabric woven by the Creole people. It is in these tales from the bayou that one finds the DNA of a place unlike any other, where the lines between the seen and unseen blur, and where the past is always present, humming a tune that is as haunting as it is beautiful.

So it remains that as long as the bayou weaves through the land, and the people of Louisiana carry forward their traditions, the lore of the bayou will continue to enchant, educate, and unify. Sustained through retelling, shared at gatherings, and ingrained in cultural rituals, these stories will always remain an integral aspect of Creole identity—a treasure trove of folklore and myth as enduring as the bayou itself.

Voodoo and Catholicism: Spiritual Syncretism As we delve into the intricate tapestry of Louisiana's Creole culture, we come upon a remarkable blending of religious traditions, namely Voodoo and Catholicism. This fusion, known as spiritual syncretism, is a result of the historical interweaving of African, European, and Indigenous spiritual practices, particularly in New Orleans.

The origin of Voodoo in Louisiana can be traced back to the arrival of enslaved Africans. These individuals carried with them their religious beliefs and practices, which included Vodou, a religion with deep roots in West African spirituality. As these enslaved people were often forced to convert to Christianity, specifically Catholicism, by their European masters, the two belief systems began to intertwine in the New World.

Voodoo's relationship with Catholicism in Louisiana is complex and multifaceted. The enslaved Africans saw similarities between their Vodou deities, known as Loa, and the Catholic saints. Over time, these Loa became associated with specific saints. For example, the loa Papa Legba, the gatekeeper of the spirit world, was often identified with Saint Peter, the keeper of the keys to heaven in Catholic tradition.

This blending went beyond just identification of spirits with saints. Rituals and ceremonies from both religions merged seamlessly. Catholic masses and Voodoo ceremonies often shared characteristics, such as the use of candles, incense, and holy water. Music and chanting were integral to both, albeit with different melodies and languages. This syncretism allowed enslaved Africans to continue practicing their ancestral spirituality under the guise of Catholic rituals.

It's important to recognize that while there are parallels and shared elements between Voodoo and Catholicism, each has maintained its unique identity. Voodoo practitioners, or Vodouisants, interact with the Loa through dance, possession, and offerings, following a religious calendar that is distinct from the Catholic one, despite some overlap in commemorations.

Catholic feast days, such as All Saints' Day on November 1st and All Souls' Day on November 2nd, have been particularly significant in the syncretic relationship. Vodouisants often hold ceremonies honoring the dead around these days, creating a bridge between the two faiths' observances for the deceased.

In the practice of Voodoo, nature and the ancestors play pivotal roles, and this can also be seen woven into the fabric of Creole Catholicism. Many Catholic churches in New Orleans are adorned with images of Saint Expedite, who is viewed as a counterpart to the loa Baron Samedi, a spirit associated with the dead.

The enduring nature of this spiritual syncretism is a testament to its depth within Creole culture. It is not a superficial mixing of beliefs, but rather a profound adaptation that arose from necessity and genuine spiritual resonance. Vodouisants have found a way to reconcile the Catholic emphasis on salvation and an afterlife with their own focus on living a balanced life in harmony with the spirits.

Despite the official stance of the Catholic Church, which does not recognize Voodoo as compatible with Catholic doctrine, the grassroots blending of the two has persisted. In the pews of many a New Orleans church, one might find individuals who participate fully in the Catholic service yet privately consult with Voodoo priests and priestesses about various aspects of life.

The presence of Voodoo practices within Catholic celebrations, like the St. John's Eve ritual held on the banks of Bayou St. John, is indicative of the enduring synergy between these faiths in Creole society. Here, Catholicism's commemoration of the birth of St. John the Baptist aligns with Voodoo rituals of purification and renewal.

Religious processions in Creole communities often bear the hallmarks of spiritual syncretism, with elements such as the use of talismans, amulets, and herbal blessings, items traditionally linked to Voodoo belief, being incorporated into Catholic celebrations.

It is not uncommon for individuals deeply embedded in Creole Catholicism to have home altars that visually represent the synthesis of these spiritual practices. Catholic icons may be placed alongside Voodoo talismans, both regarded with reverence and attributed spiritual power.

This syncretism has also found its way into life passages such as birth, marriage, and death. Baptisms, weddings, and funerals might include Voodoo blessings or customs alongside Catholic rites, creating a unique ceremonial experience that reflects the full dimension of spiritual life for Louisiana Creoles.

The Voodoo Museum in New Orleans stands as a cultural institution dedicated to preserving the history and artifacts of Voodoo. It provides an educational perspective, informing both locals and tourists about the significance of this religion and its amalgamation with Catholicism in shaping Creole spirituality.

The influence of Voodoo in Catholicism within Creole culture has given rise to a distinct religious landscape in Louisiana. Veneration of the Virgin Mary, for example, has often been juxtaposed with respect for the loa Erzulie, a deity of love and beauty. These deities share characteristics of compassion and care, providing a spiritual common ground for practitioners.

As we move forward through the annals of Louisiana's Creole culture, we must appreciate the resilience and creativity embodied in this fusion of Voodoo and Catholicism. It is not merely a facet of religious practice but a fundamental aspect of daily life that shapes the worldview of many Creoles and illustrates the ongoing evolution of spirituality amid diverse influences.

Chapter 6:
The Creole Influence on Art and Literature

The rich tapestry of Creole culture has not only shaped the social and culinary realms of Louisiana but has also left an indelible mark on the region's artistic and literary landscape. As we delve into Chapter 6, we'll uncover how Creole sensibilities have infused both art and literature with vibrant palettes of experience and perspective, revealing a world where European, African, and Indigenous influences coalesce. It's within this cultural crucible that a distinct aesthetic emerged, one characterized by its nuanced storytelling and colorful imagery, where artists and authors capture the complexities of Creole identity. From the streets of New Orleans to the banks of the Mississippi, the Creole legacy unfolds, its narratives imbued with the symbolism of this multifaceted heritage, expanding the American canon and inviting a deeper appreciation of how identity and place shape the creative spirit. The influence is undeniable, as we see figures upon canvases speak to a past that is both storied and living, and prose rich with the dialects and rhythms of a people whose history is etched into every line and hue.

Creole Narratives in Southern Literature Forming an integral part of Southern literature, Creole narratives encapsulate the cultural nuances and historical complexities of Louisiana's mixed-heritage community. These stories, depicted through the lens of various authors, offer readers a vivid portrayal of a society in which European, African, and Native American influences intersect.

One cannot explore Creole narratives without acknowledging the influence of Kate Chopin, whose works are rich with Creole life. In Chopin's "The Awakening," the protagonist's struggle with her identity and societal expectations is a resonant theme, reflecting the broader Creole experience of cultural duality.

Similarly, George Washington Cable's "The Grandissimes" dissects post-colonial race relationships and the creolization of New Orleans society in a period of significant transition. His narrative intertwines familial and societal conflicts that mirror the complexities of Creole heritage.

In contemporary literature, Ernest J. Gaines carries forward this tradition with novels such as "The Autobiography of Miss Jane Pittman," illustrating the enduring legacy of Creole culture through a woman's journey from slavery to civil rights.

These narratives are not limited to works solely focused on Creole characters; they frequently arise as vital backdrops and cultural contexts in Southern literature. The Creole settings and vernacular in James Lee Burke's Dave Robicheaux series imbue the novels with a unique sense of place, enveloped in the swampy mystique of Louisiana.

Critical to these narratives is the portrayal of language. The distinctive lexicon of Louisiana Creole French serves as more than mere dialect; it becomes a character in its own right, giving voice to the Creole experience and shaping the identities of characters within these tales.

The complexities of Creole life are also evident in the portrayal of race and society. These stories delve into the Creole community's internal dynamics, exploring the gradations of social status and colorism, concepts that are uniquely nuanced within this culture.

Gender roles are a prominent topic as well, illustrated by Chopin's work, which often centers on the role of women within Creole society. The intersection of gender, race, and class in these narratives reflects upon the limitations and expectations placed upon women in this cultural context.

Creole narratives embrace a multiplicity of experiences, from the sorrow of lost heritage to the joy of communal gatherings. These stories consistently showcase the duality of preservation and assimilation, a tension that remains a cornerstone of Creole identity in literature.

The haunting beauty of Louisiana's landscapes serves as an evocative canvas for these stories, where sugarcane plantations, winding bayous, and vibrant cities are not just settings, but characters that influence the plot and the people therein.

The influence of spirituality and folklore can also be seen weaving through the fabric of Creole narratives. The amalgamation of Voodoo beliefs with Catholic principles adds a rich, yet complex layer to the understanding of life in Creole society.

Moreover, these narratives often explore the impact of historic events such as the Louisiana Purchase, the Civil War, and the Civil Rights Movement, demonstrating how these events have shaped and reshaped the contours of Creole identity across generations.

The significance of migration in Creole literature is also palpable, tracing the movements of people either within Louisiana, to other parts of the United States, or beyond. This transience highlights the adaptability of the Creole spirit, yet also reveals a longing for belonging and an inherent connection to their roots.

Creole narratives in Southern literature enrich our understanding of American culture, providing a distinctive voice that stands apart yet is fundamentally woven into the broader tapestry of American storytelling. These stories encourage reflection on the past, a deeper understanding of the present, and thoughtful anticipation of the future of Creole culture.

As readers delve into Southern literature, the Creole narratives offer a pathway not only into the minds and hearts of its characters but also into the very soul of Louisiana. They bring to the fore an intricate world where tradition and change coexist, challenging and enlightening anyone who traverses its literary landscapes.

Chapter 7:
The Future of Creole Culture

As we close this explorative journey through the rich tapestry of Louisiana's Creole culture, one may wonder what the future holds for this vibrant and unique community. The forces of globalization and modernity continually exert their influence, but the Creole spirit, deeply rooted in its history and traditions, remains resilient. This culture, shaped by a myriad of influences, stands today as a testament to the enduring power of identity and heritage in the face of ever-evolving societal landscapes.

Language, as discussed, serves as the cornerstone of Creole culture. Louisiana Creole French persists in the face of challenges, with initiatives aimed at revitalizing this critical piece of the cultural puzzle. While the number of fluent speakers may be dwindling, there is a growing movement, particularly among the youth, to reclaim and celebrate this linguistic heritage. Efforts in education and media, alongside community programs, are honing in on preserving and proliferating this melodious dialect for future generations.

The culinary world, too, evolves, but Creole cuisine's influence continues to ripple far beyond its origins. Culinary traditions are being passed down through family lines, and innovative chefs are infusing contemporary techniques with traditional flavors. The fusion of old and new ensures the longevity of Creole cuisine while constantly reinvigorating its appeal. Food, undeniably, remains one of the most accessible and beloved ambassadors of Creole culture.

Musical expressions, such as Zydeco and Cajun, are experiencing a renaissance of interest. With festivals, dance halls, and digital platforms offering a stage for these genres, the rhythmic heart of Creole culture beats strong. The unyielding joy and communal spirit of Creole music continue to gain recognition and admirers, securing its place in the pantheon of American music culture.

Creole folklore and spirituality, a blend of the mystical and the sacred, maintain their enigmatic allure. This dimension of Creole culture, while perhaps less visible to the wider world, serves as the spiritual undercurrent that sustains the community's connection to their past and to each other. As modernity encroaches, these traditions adapt, ensuring that they remain relevant and cherished.

Art and literature, having been enriched by Creole narratives, highlight the depth and diversity of this culture's contribution to the broader American tapestry. Artists and writers with Creole roots continue to draw from their heritage, and in doing so, keep the nuances of this culture in the public eye. This enduring artistic presence is essential for the transmission and evolution of Creole culture.

Looking ahead, the dynamic nature of Creole culture suggests that it will not only survive but thrive. It has, throughout history, demonstrated an outstanding ability to adapt while maintaining its core identity. As the world changes, Creole culture will likely continue to absorb new influences and reflect them in ways that are both innovative and respectful of its rich heritage.

Educational initiatives remain pivotal for the perpetuation of Creole culture. There is an increasing emphasis on the inclusion of Creole history and practices in educational materials and institutions. By embedding Creole studies in the curriculum, the younger generation will be equipped with knowledge and pride in their origins, enabling them to carry the torch forth.

Technology, too, plays a fundamental role in the transmission of culture in the modern era. Social media and digital platforms offer unprecedented opportunities for sharing and preserving Creole culture. From online repositories of Creole music and folklore to virtual cooking classes celebrating Creole cuisine, these tools empower the Creole community to maintain connectivity and promote their culture on a global scale.

The challenges facing Creole culture are complex and multifaceted. Urbanization, economic hardship, and environmental issues, particularly in the Southern Louisiana region, are pressing concerns. As the Creole community grapples with these trials, their collective resilience and ingenuity will be crucial assets.

The essence of Creole culture lies in its communal bonds and the shared experiences that define this group. The future of this culture depends on the engagement of community members and their commitment to fostering a sense of identity and belonging within the next generation. Community events, family gatherings, and religious practices serve as vital arenas where cultural transmission occurs organically.

Tourism plays a double-edged role in the evolution of Creole culture. While it brings attention and economic benefits, there is also a risk of commodification and distortion. Navigating this landscape requires a careful balance, one that promotes authentic representation and economic sustainability without sacrificing the culture's integrity.

Environmental change, particularly, presents a significant challenge. Creole culture is inextricably linked to the land and waterways of Louisiana, which face threats from climate change and natural degradation. Environmental stewardship is more crucial than ever for the protection of the geographical bedrock of this vibrant culture.

Ultimately, the future of Creole culture will be defined by a continually evolving conversation between the past and the present. As new voices emerge and older ones pass on the baton, the dialogue will undoubtedly shift, accommodating contemporary realities while treasuring an irreplaceable heritage. Creole culture is a living, breathing entity, poised for transformation yet anchored by an unbreakable lineage.

In summary, the landscape that lies ahead for Louisiana's Creole culture is one of opportunity intertwined with challenges. The vitality and passion that have characterized the Creole people for centuries are the same strengths that will propel them into the future. With each spoken word of Louisiana Creole French, each savored dish of gumbo, each note played on the accordion, and each tale told under the bayou moon, Creole culture continues its remarkable narrative, embracing tomorrow without ever letting go of yesterday.

www.ingramcontent.com/pod-product-compliance
Lightning Source LLC
Chambersburg PA
CBHW050342290526
45785CB00006B/2599